How to Upsize Your Career

by

Marty Morris

How to Upsize Your Career

Cover art by Stephen J. F. Neubauer

ISBN 1-932196-56-0

One Night Books
#2

WordWright.biz

P.O. Box 1785
Georgetown, TX 78627

Printed in the United States of America

This book is dedicated to you, the working person. I've been where you are now, or may be in the near future: downsized, laid off, terminated without cause; in other words, without a job.

I believe what you're about to read will help you. My suggestions are based on first-hand experiences. Be advised, though. Nothing is going to happen unless you decide to take the first step, namely, reading this book.

Marty Morris
Midland, Texas 2005

Table of Contents

Introduction

Whether you're entering the job market, worked there for a time, or remain a seasoned veteran in the work-a-day-world, you must read this book. You'll find something you can use, whether currently employed, or like thousands of others, wishing you had a job.

The past few years should have convinced you that almost everything you took for granted has disappeared. Longevity, a concept of the past, now means days or perhaps weeks. Financial strength can disappear with tomorrow morning's national newscast. You must provide personal security for the people close to you.

Despite all these problems, I can help. I know you want answers, and I know I can provide them. You'll find the wisdom here, and perhaps help others with their questions.

Chapter 1

The Show Begins

Whether fueled by rumors or hints of corporate scandals, large-scale layoffs, firings and downsizings have circulated for weeks. Things you haven't thought about for years come to mind. Did I do what they expected of me? Did I dress right? Did I miss deadlines? Did I do anything wrong? What if my job goes away? What about my family? Will I have a retirement? Will I get my next paycheck? Do I still know how to get a job?

Your phone rings and your manager wants to see you. Upon arriving, your manager smiles grimly and asks you to take a seat. You then spot the personnel manager seated across the room. You have clammy hands and weak knees. Breathing just got a little harder. You have a knot in your throat and can't speak.

"I'm sorry, but I have unpleasant news," your manager begins. "I'm sure you know we recently reviewed our current and future business objectives with a keen eye toward reducing expenses and preparing for future ventures and opportunities. With that in mind, I sincerely regret that we no longer need your services. This decision does not reflect on your performance; as always you provided exemplary service. Simply put, your job no longer exists. We will give you a very favorable recommendation and wish you the best in your future endeavors."

Short, shocking, to the point, and in accordance with EEOC guidelines, your job no longer exists. Years of hard work mean nothing. Your career has come to an abrupt halt. Following a deafening silence of a few seconds, and without an invitation, you stand and leave the room without comment.

When the door closes, you experience a brief sense of relief. Now, where do you go? Perhaps back to your old workstation or office, to gather your personal items, before security personnel escort you off company property? While the shock hasn't worn off, you need to deal with a few things right now. The job you had thirty minutes ago, your career, and a large number of your life expectations have popped like a soap bubble.

If this has happened to you already, it will likely happen again soon. Like a top 40 hit, it makes the play list more than we like. Downsizing, termination, rightsizing, corporate weight trimming, realignment, reorganization, all mean hit the road Jack.

At the same time, we've also had our attention directed to the welfare and future of the company, firm, organization or business entity affected. *Oh, poor company! What will they do now?*

What about the person whose job doesn't exist

anymore? What happens to him or her now? Eventually, the focus shifts to the individual, but not soon enough.

I wrote this book for the seasoned working professional. However, recent entrants to the job market (whether formally educated or not) will also find helpful suggestions to begin their professional careers. It provides a weather guide for our current storms, a *Farmers Almanac* for career planning. For currently working professionals with several years experience, downsized former employees, or new job market entrants, I will emphasize the importance of careful and thorough research into new professional opportunities.

Successive chapters and exercises discuss and suggest ways to take charge of your professional destiny that will enhance (upsize) your skills, and thereby your employability, and not paint yourself into a professional corner (downsize your employability.)

Because of the ongoing interest in career establishment and enhancement based on this title and focus, several exercises and a suggested reading list enhance the text.

Chapter 2

Hey! I'm Still Working

Congratulations! You might still have a job. However, don't take life too easy. You still have plenty to do. As granny said, "Make hay while the sun shines!" Keep reading and start planning. Your company decided to downsize for various reasons, such as:

- reduced market demand
- to reduce expenses, and/or improve the profit margin.
- unfavorable rulings from government agencies or courts.
- eliminate unprofitable or marginally profitable lines.
- prepare the company for a merger, acquisition or leveraged buy out (LBO)[1].

---

[1] Boockholdt, J. L., Ph. D. & Robert W. Service, Ph. D. *Strategies For Individual Survival During a Corporate Consolidation.* Corpus Christi, TX: Society for Advancement of Management, Aut., 1997.

If they didn't catch you in this downsizing, take some immediate actions to prepare yourself for the next round. Depending upon your situation, you might only have a few weeks to react. You might also have up to a year, but even one year doesn't provide much time to prepare for the rest of your working life. Invest your time and money wisely.

The following suggestions provide a starting point. You'll probably think of others better suited to your needs. Make these your catalysts for the next few weeks.

Exercise 2-1:
Here's What I Want To Do While I Still Can

This exercise helps you think about the present, what you've done, and to consider your future. For this exercise, assume you have all the resources (money, time, land, youth, family support, great health, good looks, etc.) you need.

You might amaze yourself at the number of things you'll write down. Keep plenty of blank paper and pencils close by. Allow yourself an uninterrupted hour in a quiet place away from other people. Write the date at the top of each page, and then write what you want to do before you die.

Once you start, don't stop and don't edit. Keep writing. NO EVALUATIONS ALLOWED! Save everything!

This should really tire you out. Keep at it until you

run out of energy. When you feel "spent," put your pencil down. Walk away from this and don't touch it for a few days. Do something else. Read a book or magazine. Ride a bicycle. Swim. Take a hike. Clean windows, bathroom tubs or floors. Watch movies. Cook something. Walk a mile. Do your laundry.

After a couple of days, read what you wrote. Don't pick up a pencil. Read every word. Visualize whatever comes to mind as you read.

Only then may you issue opinions about what you wrote. Don't start ripping each item apart yet. Let these freewheeling suggestions sink in.

After another day or so, you'll conclude you really can achieve some of your wishes you thought you never would.

Here's What I Want to Do While I Still Can

(To keep these pages from remaining blank, YOU have to complete them!)

Educational Inventory

Should you complete your degree? How much time and money will it require? Do you need an advanced degree, or perhaps a degree in another field?

Wait a minute! You've gotten older. If you left school 15 - 20 years ago, another Bachelor's or Master's degree won't really do much for your remaining working years. Watch out for the school trap. (Men age 40-45 have a big problem and fill many MBA programs.) Think about why school may trap you:

- It might take 2 - 6 years to complete.
- An advanced degree may require full-time attendance on campus for at least the final year.
- Your out-of-pocket costs will probably range between $10,000 and $20,000.
- If you pursue it full-time, you may deplete your savings.
- As rapidly as skills requirements change today, you may have chosen the wrong degree program after spending one to two years on it and a lot of money.
- Some other options you should consider include:
  - Attending computer-oriented applications seminars.
  - Learning to build and maintain spreadsheets.
  - Learning to use desktop publishing and computer graphics software.
  - Learning to use relational databases.

Whether or not you currently work in computer operations or programming activities, you must learn more about computers than you currently know. Attend classes offered by local community and associate colleges, or national software training companies to upgrade your personal computer literacy. Not only will this require less time than a university degree program, it won't cost as much. You can also add your fellow students and instructors to your networking group.

Sometimes, training departments have the responsibility for outplacement assistance for downsized employees. It doesn't mean they will find the downsized employee a new job. Rather, they will offer advice and counsel about the most effective job search techniques. However, don't count on this. The size of the company and their degree of "community conscience" usually determines if they offer outplacement assistance.

If the Training Department remains alive and well, learn as soon as possible what (re)training opportunities they offer. If management hasn't selected your department or job for future elimination, you might have time to retrain for a more valuable skill before the next downsizing wave occurs.

If your current employer will give you the time and money to attend any course, no matter what the subject, take it.

Get Certified (CPA, CIA, CDP, CISA, CBA, PE)

Does your employer recognize, encourage and hopefully pay for such designations? Maybe you can earn certification easier than you think. Your earlier degree(s), along with another in-service, correspondence, or continuing education courses could qualify you for relatively low cost and little time.

Most companies consider certified employees more valuable because they have more experience to draw from compared to non-certified employees. Additionally, the company can advertise their certified staff when seeking new or repeat business. You may feel certification just represents a magic word for something you already know, and have avoided the process. Well, my friend, words have magic, try the sound of, "You're hired."

Certification programs come from professional organizations in many fields including accounting, financial planning, internal auditing, career placement, law, data processing, engineering, insurance, computers, medicine, dentistry, and environmental science. Searching the Internet or a visiting your local library will help you find which organizations offer such programs, what they cost, how to enroll, and when the examinations take place.

If you already work with computer systems operating software, then perhaps acquiring a designation as a Certified Network Engineer should follow.[2] Some software training companies and vendors offer such certification courses and seminars at various locations around the country. Check your telephone company's phone book for local listings.

Depending upon your type of work, consider holding a license in that field to enhance your security and employability. Some companies have ways around this, but their exception won't make or save your career.

Some effort on your part could better insulate you from a potentially difficult situation, should you fall victim to downsizing in the future. Call your state's

---

[2] Vitiello, Jill. *Badge of Glory*. Computerworld, February 16, 1998, pg. 77.

occupational licensing office to find out if your field requires licensing. If so, learn what books you need; forms to complete; what work experiences and validations they need, and what examinations you must pass to obtain the license.

A word of caution: if your employer hasn't made you aware of state-issued license requirements, they might not look favorably upon your efforts to acquire one. Cautiously inquire where you stand before announcing your intentions.

On the other hand, your employer may not only pay for such an effort, but may provide the additional on-the-job training you need to acquire the license. Discretion can help you stay employed.

Finally, don't overlook re-certification. If you already hold a certification, designation or license, contact the issuing organization about re-certification programs. Determine if you need to re-certify. How long does the re-certification period last? How do you re-certify yourself? How much does it cost? Have they created new provisions for re-certification since your last certification? If so, who does it affect? Once successfully re-certified, how will the public know? Will your name appear in a licensing authority directory, or must you toot your own re-certified horn?

Offer Ideas

Does your company have a suggestion program? If so, determine when your ideas save you and when they sink you. Begin by learning about the suggestion program. How does the process start? Find out what happens to the paper that flows through the system. Who sees the forms? Who evaluates them? Who rates the proposed suggestions? Who determines the award levels? Who recognizes the successful employee and in what form? i.e., money, award certificate, merchandise, paid time off, honorable mention, etc.? Don't give your company a ten million dollar idea for a nifty pen-and-pencil set. The editor of my book told me he once got a small plaque that announced he had saved his corporation a quarter of a million dollars. This didn't save him from rightsizing, but it might have if he had gained real recognition for his ideas.

Looking for areas of improvement can require lots of time, questions, research, analysis, and even lots of rejection and disappointment. To succeed, persist, research thoroughly, document well, and draw clear conclusions in dollars and cents.

Before you start telling others about how the company can save time and effort or make more money, acquaint yourself with other areas of the firm. Don't tell your company how to eliminate your job! Determine where your efforts fit into the overall process.

This research activity will help you learn. You may discover you have little value to the overall production cycle. If so, don't let that deter you from discovering more about your company. Learn more about why the company does what it does. Can you obtain a list of company customers? What companies supply your company? Does the company have an exclusive on the items they produce, or do they share the market with competitors? What affects the company's services and products?

What levels of customer satisfaction has your company achieved with its customers? Can you identify needed improvements with production, transportation or final delivery processes? If so, at what cost and benefit? Get excited about your research. Unless you have enthusiasm for what your company does, you'll soon find yourself on the chopping block. The, "It's only a crappy job," attitude leads to, "Which way to the unemployment office?"

Looking into such areas should excite you and provide valuable insight about how your company operates. However, you probably want to err on the side of caution regarding how much you talk about what you see. Observe everything you can. Make written notes if you need to (after you leave the immediate area in question.) Ask questions if you can do so without drawing undue attention to yourself. Sometime later, reflect on and analyze what you observed. Make hand drawings to understand complex processes.

Familiarizing yourself with company operations with the idea of suggesting improvements will let you come face-to-face with the political realities of making suggestions. Someone else may have already suggested what you intend to offer, and has the political clout to push their suggestion(s) ahead of yours. Unfortunately, that's how suggestion programs generally work, even though you won't find any written rules documenting this. If you find this kind of opposition, consider how, or if, you will proceed. If you think management might not eliminate your job during the next downsizing, you probably don't want to upset the senior staff with an unexpected intrusion into a company operation outside your immediate area.

How much do you know about laws regarding copyrights, trademarks, trade secrets, or service marks? Know the rules and regulations before you make a suggestion concerning intellectual property. Get on the Internet or visit your local library, and review the publications that govern new ideas, inventions, and processes.

You'll need to understand your company's requirements for confidentiality of company information and conflicts of interest regarding suggestions. Even with all your research and diligence, you may unknowingly cut yourself out of substantial royalties, copyrights or trade agreements. However, if you have a case to present, seek some competent legal advice on related issues.

As you research such conflicts of interest, determine if your current job description calls for you to look for improved work methods or processes in your immediate area(s) of responsibility. If so, look into other company activities for your suggestions.

Take a Good Look at Yourself

At the Greek temple at Delphi sat a polished bronze mirror with the words beneath it "Know Thyself!" Twenty six hundred years ago the Greeks knew that people judge you by your looks. Not surprisingly, we do too.

Reexamine your dress attire, speech mannerisms and vocal patterns. Consider changing your appearance. While such advice may sound worn out, it impacts how others perceive you. Perform your job so others can clearly see your professional performance and appearance.

Your type of business usually determines how you dress at work. If you drive a delivery truck and carry items to a customer's facility, repair equipment on-site, or perform maintenance activities, then choose casual clothing, a uniform, or protective clothing.

If you meet with the public, wear appropriate business attire. You can make adjustments if necessary. Just don't make those changes on your own. Your client should suggest them first, otherwise ask for the guidelines and when you have the option, exercise them. You can't start Hawaiian shirt day alone!

Many offices now accept "business casual." However, put on a tie, a sport coat, business jacket or blouse, perhaps a pair of business shoes, just in case you get called into a meeting with clients or company executives. If you need a model to guide you in choosing a style of dress, look at business clothing ads in your local newspaper, particularly the Sunday newspaper. They set the pace, whether you like their style choices or not.

Determine the acceptable dress code, style, or norms in your area. Keep your hair neatly groomed or coiffed. For males, go for a clean-shaven face or neatly trimmed beard, mustache or sideburns. Look like a slightly better groomed version of your boss.

For females, choose traditional hairstyles that compliment your face, apparel and accessories. Long, flowing, over-the-shoulder hairstyles may not work at this time. For questions about dress codes, seek outside professional advice and counsel.

If you need glasses or hearing aids, make sure they compliment your dress style and know how to use them quickly and efficiently. Don't fumble with them. If you need your glasses to read, put them on at the beginning of the activity and don't take them off. Adjust your hearing aid when conversations with others begin. Try not to make adjustments later in your exchanges. However, should you need to make adjustments, make them without drawing undue attention to yourself.

Conservative colors, stripes, and prints in two or three-piece suits and dresses always remain in style and reflect good taste. You can't go wrong if you choose white shirts with tasteful, but conservative neckties.

Traditional accessory items like wedding rings, high school or college class rings, watches, conservative necklaces, earrings, cufflinks, add to your look. However, if you want to create a favorable impression, stay away from items or colors that draw undue attention such as flashy jewelry, beads, caps, headwear, studded ear pins, or penny loafers.

Choose skirt lengths at or below knee level. Clean, neatly pressed shirts, pants, blouses, and skirts, as well as conservatively designed shoes, socks, and hosiery will charm people with your thoughtfulness. If you dress for your office, you reflect the good aspects of the company's culture like a mirror.

Do others think of you as articulate? Can you find the right word for every situation? If not, read some of the excellent books available for improving your word power. You'll have fun with this and enhance your self-confidence, as well as learn to think more clearly.

What kinds of jokes or humorous comments do you pass on? Do others always react positively to them? Do others misinterpret your comments? Do you need to listen more and comment less? Good listeners make people feel better. Look through the suggested reading list at the end of this book for some publications on grammar and language.

Universities and continuing education programs, as well as correspondence courses, provide several formal options to improve these skills. You can find them on the Internet, as well as your local library, high schools, and university locations in your area.

Does speaking in front of others terrify you? If so, admit you need to speak better and find a nearby Toastmaster's International Club to visit and see how they can help you. Most people fear public speaking more than death, and few realize what an important job skill it provides.

Are You a Team Member?

If you haven't worked in a team before, find ways to do so. Teams perform more efficiently, and a team of eight can often do the work of twelve lone wolves. To do this, you need certain skills.

The lone worker used to represent the backbone of American business: dedicated, daring, hard working. Now employers consider them a possible problem. What if he fails or gets sick? Who understands what she does? Maybe he has a non-corporate agenda.

Team members need good interpersonal skills when working with peers and management personnel. How do you measure up? Do your co-workers respect you as a team member? Do you willingly listen to others and work for the good of the team, or do you always feel others must accept your suggestions? Do you respect the concept of *creative compromise*? Can you compromise and contribute to group goals or do you prefer being *right*, no matter the consequences?

If becoming a team member seems strange, consider the following ideas. Suggest new procedures, systems, or products and organize your team as the most qualified to produce them. Propose a team approach to solving major or recurring problems in the company. Make sure you have an approach to solve the issue, not just to identify problems. Look for opportunities to train others in the job(s) you've previously performed. Demonstrate how to perform them easier or more efficiently.

If you began your working career as a member of a

team or project, you probably work easily in such an environment and shouldn't experience serious difficulties moving from one project to another. However, if you only have one or two specific skills, or have pursued a *lone wolf* work environment, you should prepare yourself for a major cultural change in the workplace.

Team members possess several skills to make their projects successful: good technical and/or administrative skills, good interpersonal traits, strong organizational skills, and the companion abilities to speak and write well. Listening skills remain critically important to the team and the individuals on the team. Do you really listen? Find out what your co-workers and supervisors think about your open-mindedness. Ask them to honestly discuss the issue with you. Learn to make some adjustments in how you listen to others.

Team membership does not mean you have vanished from view. In fact, it means the opposite because more people know and depend on you. The effective employee shines in this world. As a team member, you'll contribute to the team's efforts on a regular basis. You'll quantify your contributions and results: how many hours of production time your team saved; how many hours or days ahead of schedule your team achieved results; how much money your team saved; how much more profit the company realized as a result of what your team accomplished. Team members spread the workload among several people. However, becoming a team member also implies the need to work smarter, not necessarily harder, to insure that your contributions shine.

Watch Out for Rumors

When rumors about downsizings, layoffs, cutbacks, and job eliminations circulate, employees talk about what they've heard. Don't join in. If rumors circulating through unofficial channels affect other people, turn your head the other way, or walk away from the discussion. This way you'll avoid a lot of trouble. Gossip, an addictive pastime, can put you out of work. E-mail gossip can really backfire because someone can read every word you type and when the downsizing comes, they will.

Company grapevines generally know what's going to happen long before the events takes place. You'll find it very difficult to avoid listening to the buzz discussed over the cubicle walls, in the break room, or in the parking lot. Acting on gossip may mean you unwittingly do someone else's bidding.

Despite the company's grapevine, make sure your comments remain factual, authentic, and business related. While your position might make you privy to confidential information, such exposure doesn't give you the right to broadcast it

Keep focused on your professional future. Remember, whether you remain with your current employer for a long time or not, your reputation follows you like a shadow.

What if the rumor links you directly to the event or action? What now? Do you ignore it and go about your business as though nothing happened? Perhaps. You'll have to make a judgment call.

If you decide to take no immediate action, make sure your subsequent responses and comments reflect your decision. However, if you must respond, quickly discover the source of the information and confront those responsible for passing on the information. You won't enjoy this, but it could save your job.

Most rumors, when tracked down, remain unfounded, or grossly exaggerated. If you track down a true one and it affects you directly, then you must decide what to do. Do you stay with this company or leave? What's in your best interest? Should you cut your losses and move on? Weigh your options and make a decision.

If you leave the company voluntarily, secure several letters of reference from current and former supervisors BEFORE you leave. After you depart, phone calls and requests for reference letters often fall on deaf ears.

Timing Is Everything

Do you arrive late, leave early, and stretch your lunch periods and breaks by a few minutes each day? Then your head will likely land on the chopping block. It doesn't matter that you provide excellent work, because management will make you an easy target when they must come up with a certain number of heads.

If your punctuality comes under review, consider some changes in your use of time. Arrive at work a little earlier and leave a little later. Consider taking your breaks at your work location, or perhaps not taking them at all.

Let these changes reflect a difference in the way you work and use the extra time for the company's benefit. Use this extra time to work on a special project, like the one to help the company make or save some money. But don't only do; *make sure management knows you do.*

Don't overlook the time it takes to complete your tasks. Often we work well on projects and forget the incidentals that slow us down. The best-made report sitting in the copy center for hours doesn't help your reputation. Look for ways to shave a little time off the project such as hand-delivering results instead of depending on office mail delivery; using e-mail or fax instead of written correspondence; using the Internet as an additional source of reference material, and writing your own memos on the department word processor instead of depending on the steno pool or office secretary.

The wagons have circled the big subject of time management. No matter how well you think you manage time, you can always make some change and get a little more of that precious and sometimes elusive commodity. Local bookstores and mail order firms contain several good books on time management. Look in the Business or Self Help sections. Don't overlook the weekly business magazines. They contain many advertisements about instructor-led time management seminars, as well as mail order correspondence courses.

Do you write down your scheduled activities before you begin working on them? If not, start doing it and make it a part of your daily routine. Work on your most important projects and activities first. Decide which one needs your attention first. What's next? Can you eliminate or delay some activities? The tired old saw of "Work Smarter Not Harder" still rings true in today's job climate.

You've begun to set priorities, an important part of managing your time. If you've taken a few minutes and effort to set priorities for how you'll use your time, then stick to it! Go after the most important projects first and move on to the next.

Use your travel time to and from work to listen to audio training tapes. Perhaps you can read about your new field or skill while riding public transportation. Make the best use of your time.

What about those nights in a motel, away from the office and your family? Don't waste your time catching up on the latest TV episode. Pick up a book, turn on your tape recorder with a "Book On Tape," or WRITE!

A Day's Work for a Day's Pay

If you didn't lose your job in the first downsizing wave, remember the above title, and prepare for a few changes such as:

- Your employer will likely ask you to take on some additional responsibilities and tasks, which belonged to downsized colleagues.
- You may receive a new or additional job title for which you won't likely receive any money. You'll hear explanations like "keeping costs in line," or "corporate belt-tightening."

- Your next personnel evaluation may have glowing words with little or no raise in pay.

You'll hear promises like, "We'll make it up to you next year." Such promises have little value. While the explanations may reflect truth, these actions should alert your internal radar network. Your professional career rests in the balance. You may need to work another 10 to 30 years. Changes in your current work environment, like those described above, will likely happen. For the moment, begin learning new skills, make better use of your time and energy, and forget the notion that the company will take care of you. Praise often wafts like a gentle breeze before a storm, like the cool summer breeze in the afternoon before a hailstorm.

Your employer will provide a salary and some benefits as long as you provide valuable work. The instant management perceives you no longer provide this, your continued employment will soon end.

How about using the power curve in your favor? Don't wait to take on new or additional responsibilities. Volunteer! Keep in mind the image you'll create in the minds of the company's supervisors and managers. If the initial suggestion comes from you, it can provide the perfect time to talk with your supervisor about that special project you've wanted to pursue. If they accept, you can work on something that interests you, instead of dealing with someone's leftover ideas.

Does your company have a "hotshot?" You know, someone who keeps it all together and gets an enormous amount of work done? What's their secret? No secret at all, simply good work habits, habits you can copy yourself.

According to William L. Ayers, founder and president of the New York-based Ayers Group, "Those who can bridge their technical and managerial ability with good organizational and people skills will see their career shift into high gear."[3]

Do you perform at a top level? Consider these tips to help you improve:

- Always work in sync with your organization's business plan. Gear your efforts to achieving well-defined goals.
- Dedicate yourself to producing measurable results. Management will judge you by your contributions and your desire to take on extra projects.
- Pitch good ideas to people who have the power to implement them.
- Set goals that rise above the prevailing expectations.
- Engage others in your ideas and success.
- Seek formal training and mentors or coaches to develop your skills

---

[3] Ayers, William L. *How to Be a Top Performer*. Beyond Computing, Jan/Feb 1998, pg. 16.

Chapter 3

I'm Still Being Downsized!

Despite all your hard work, the company may still let you go with very little notice. Determine the real reason for your termination. If economic, you may decide to leave your field or your region. If you did something wrong, you must change your habits and get the embarrassing fact behind you.

Get ready for your next position by learning which corporate functions management wants eliminated. This will help you focus over the next few weeks.

No matter your organizational position in the company, ask your supervisor or manager what outplacement counseling exists for downsized employees at your level. Ask as though you expect it. If they will provide such counseling, then you'll know soon enough if you'll receive the outplacement services.

If the company hasn't thought about providing outplacement counseling, your question comes at the right time. Companies don't always provide counseling, but their public image shines more if they provide outplacement counseling or retraining.

Unfortunately, you can easily fall into a trap. On the one hand, you know your company's downsizing people in large numbers. On the other hand, you know you provide valuable talents. Maybe someone in senior management knows this as well.

Really? Wake up!

No guardian angel at your company will save you. Most everyone experiences this denial because losing a job creates tremendous stress topped only by the death of a spouse. We respond by telling ourselves lies and inventing stories that make us feel better. Don't do this. Heed the alarm bells and attack the problem with wide-open eyes.

Use your remaining time wisely and learn the truth and determine your future. You and only you can do this, a sobering and frightening thought.

Start directing questions to the right people. Don't take no for an answer. What's the worst that could happen? Lose your job? That has already happened.

A word of caution, don't *demand* any information. The company may have a legitimate and legal right not to reveal certain information. However, make a written note of the date, place, time, person talked with, and the exact responses.

Consider this tip. If you start asking questions about the plans the company has for you, keep your notepad and pencil close by. Write things down. Don't commit them to memory. Doing this has two advantages:

- You can accurately record what you hear.

- The other party or parties to your conversation will likely speak honestly and directly in a quiet measured manner.

By the way, if they ask you not to take notes, leave, walk away, exit, and otherwise refuse to participate. If you stay, you're guaranteed to lose, then make a written note of this event.

I haven't discussed communications with family members. Your job loss stresses them too.

Your family or significant other(s) have probably figured out the situation on their own, and without you having said a word. You're an open book to them. Even so, tell them what's going on, as least as much as you understand. Talking with someone close to you has the following advantages:

- It takes some pressure off you.
- They can suggest something you hadn't previously thought of.

Now we'll examine the importance of understanding your emotional barometer.

Emotional Barometer

A barometer measures atmospheric pressure or elevation and gives notice of fluctuations. What about an emotional barometer? Does it measure or sense pressure or fluctuations? Probably, but not in terms we normally deal with. You may find this difficult to quantify. When a job loss happens, our individual emotional roller coasters speed up significantly. In many cases, emotions can go out of control. It begins with a sense of no control over your own life followed by denial, rage, and distraction behaviors.

Before you lost your job, what did you think about? What did you think about your performance? Did you do everything you could have on your last few projects and deliver the best possible results? Did you find obstacles beyond your control that prevented you from completing your objective? If so, what? If you didn't complete your last assignment, why not? Did you record your contributions to the project? Can you prove these assertions? Even so, will it matter?

What satisfied you most about your former job? What aspects about it made you feel the most frustrated?

If the company hadn't downsized you, what kept you there? Money? Job security? Job satisfaction? Work schedule? Peer relationships? Benefits? Start writing these things down, now!

Did your former job serve only to keep the real world away? Did you say or do something that drew unfavorable attention to you?

Were you intolerant or short with people, who had enjoyed your civility and cordiality in the past? Did you say *strange, weird,* or *out of character* things? Did you have any odd behaviors? Have you asked your former colleagues about your last days and weeks at work?

Don't think of these questions as unimportant, not related, or things you don't need to deal with now. Guess what? You do! You probably did some things in your earlier job you should never do again.

What made your last job so meaningful/wonderful that you didn't change jobs several months ago? Don't put off answering this question; address it now. You may not like the answers, but at least you'll know the truth.

It may be difficult to deal with the past, particularly if your previous actions determined where you find yourself now. Face whatever demons dwell there, and get past them. Now we'll measure your emotional barometer and determine if it's increasing or decreasing. No matter which, you need to control it.

Perhaps you should cut your losses. Difficult? Yes. However, you must get past what has happened, face the future and grow as a result of the experience.

Dr. Daniel Goleman suggests you may need to rely on your Emotional Quotient, or EQ.[4] Goleman defines EQ as the power to both perceive and control emotions.

Goleman confirms what common sense has long observed: success requires more than a high IQ. Laughing at the boss's jokes, trusting co-workers with confidences, and recognizing when someone teeters on the verge of a nervous breakdown represent a form of smarts every bit as vital to workplace survival as understanding the electoral college, knowing how to do cube roots, or knowing how to change a flat.

According to Goleman, EQ has the following dimensions:

- knowing one's emotions and controlling them

---

[4] Goleman, Daniel, Ph. D. *Emotional Intelligence.* New York: Bantam Books, 1995.

- recognizing and sharing emotions in others (empathy)
- self-motivation

What Not to Do

Don't start thinking of yourself as having nothing to do. Family and friends will try to cheer you up, and you can let weeks go by watching TV, going to movies or puttering in the yard. It feels less stressful until you max out the credit card!

Don't waste your time repainting the house or sharpening your golf game. Watch out for stress overload. Other issues in your life will demand your attention such as a child with problems in school, or perhaps an aging parent's illness. Therefore, concentrate your thought and focus on those major involvements over which you do have significant control. Postpone taking on a major financial commitment, such as buying a new car, or campaigning for a community leadership position.

Don't burn your bridges. While letting off steam reportedly reduces stress, current research doesn't support this approach. Common sense dictates you shouldn't alienate people who can help with a successful career search.

Not many years ago, a stigma attached itself to someone who lost a job through layoff or job elimination. In the 1950s and 1960s people treated them like lepers. But today, people understand it happens every day.

Do you talk with anyone about your emotional barometric pressures? Who? A family member? A former professional colleague? A neighbor? A personal friend? While talking with these people about your situation may feel right, it may not give you the therapeutic relief or necessary advice you need.

You might need some professional advice from a counselor, psychologist, or even a psychiatrist. Don't reject your family members or friends as sources for information or advice. However, a trained professional might recognize the symptoms you exhibit and perhaps spot a problem quicker, or offer a different approach others may not easily see.

You might experience a midlife crisis while you go through a job change. Dr. Daniel Levinson, a Yale University Professor and Psychologist states, "Many people who make an occupational choice early, say that by around age 30 that they made a mistake. If they really focus on that and stay with the question – 'What kind of occupation is best for me?' – it's possible to make a change . . . and do satisfying, productive work."[5]

Dr Levinson continues, "The problem isn't just to get over a midlife crisis but to get through it. It's important to get clear what's wrong with their lives. People need to spend more time exploring what's happening, and what it is they are feeling, rather than to jump right away to an action."

When asked about coping with Midlife Crisis, Dr.

---

[5] *Midlife Crisis – Is It Unavoidable?* U. S. News & World Report, October 25, 1982.

Levinson responded, ". . . it helps to know that you're not alone and that you're struggling with issues that are part of the human life cycle. But a midlife crisis isn't like having a cold. It isn't something that will go away if you just wait it out. There's some real change in one's life that has to be made to get through a midlife crisis in a constructive way."

What Have You Done?

Though still employed, start a written list of your *accomplishments* and *achievements,* not *responsibilities.* Your next employer wants to know what you have done and what you can do, not what you used to do. Exercise 3-1 will focus on this. Before writing everything you've done since birth, cut the list down.

Perhaps you've lived in many different places because your family moved a lot. You might have attended several schools or had an idyllic upbringing in rural America. None of this matters and you should focus instead on your accomplishments.

Deciding what you have done does not include events and activities you attended as a spectator. For example, assume you went to a sporting event as a spectator. If your favorite team won or lost, the final outcome did not result from your attendance. However, if you scored the only touchdown, run, or goal to win the game, then you did it.

Employers want to hear "I designed the phone

system" not "I worked for Middle Earth Bell when they invented the hobbitphone."

If you designed and built your first playhouse, or if you wrote a poem or song at seven years old, take credit for it. You'll remember many such things from your earlier days. You'll create a sizeable list, just let it grow.

Maybe during your freshman year of Psychology 101 you thought of a way to communicate with catatonic patients. Don't discount the experience. Revisit it. We neglect the gold in the streams of our life because life distracts us. Going back to pan for gold where you found it before can help you find it again.

Something you did years ago, like help a friend with a math problem or English sentence construction could have had lasting affects on the person you helped. How will you know unless you ask?

Some elementary and high school teachers might have had a different insight about your talents, at least the talents they thought you possessed. Find them and talk with them. The experience will help you, and they will truly appreciate your efforts to locate and talk with them.

Keep several notebooks and pencils within arm's reach. Make lots of notes about what you've done over the years. If a thought comes to mind, write it down no matter how insignificant it may seem. A few days later, it may spark many new thoughts about what you actually did. Date your notepad sheets, and don't throw the notes away! They'll serve as a great audit trail. Use them to summarize your earlier days.

With this exercise you will have mapped your life,

your interests and abilities, and made yourself feel better. Begin your quest knowing you packed your bags, both emotionally and experientially. You might have trouble packing your bags, especially since you don't know how far you'll travel, so I hope you spend enough time on this exercise.

This exercise can rekindle a forgotten fire in your mind. If you were fifteen years old when you had a solution about how to finance multiple mortgages with other people's money, don't discard the idea. Use the same logic for future endeavors. Follow the steps on the next page to complete Exercise 3-1.

Exercise 3-1: What Have You Done?

Prepare a written list of your *accomplishments* and *achievements.*

- Read the list of words on the following pages and check those important to the proper performance of your current job.
- Highlight the tasks you perform.
- Using those words, begin writing about your achievements and accomplishments from previous positions. Write about the outcome in measurable, identifiable, or tangible terms.
- Show the true meaning of your achievements and accomplishments by demonstrating you can:
  - reduce turnover

- increase sales
- prevent losses
- increase productivity
- reduce absenteeism
- shorten training time/expenses
- develop new models, techniques, systems
- increase or extend knowledge
- improve the functioning of an organization
- introduce products or services to new markets

Some of the action words in the list serve only to help you focus on your accomplishments. You wouldn't want to use them in a resume. I've included them as catalysts to help you discover the things that you do well. Don't inflate or exaggerate your achievements to create a fantasy. Discover the reality of your achievements.

Action Verbs for Writing Achievements/Accomplishments

abolished
absorbed
abstracted
accelerated
accented
accepted
accessed
acclimated
accommodated
accomplished
accounted
accrued
achieved
acquired
acted
activated
added
addressed
adjusted
administered
adopted
advanced
advertised
advised
affected
aided
alerted
allowed
altered
amended
analyzed
anticipated
appealed
appeared
applied
appointed
appraised
appropriated
approved
arbitrated
arranged
ascertained
assembled
assessed
attained
audited
averted
baked
balanced
based
batched
battled
beat
began
belonged
bestowed
blasted
blew
blocked
boarded
bolstered
boosted
borrowed
bought
braced
bred
brewed
broadened
brought
brushed
buckled
budgeted
built
calculated
calibrated
called
campaigned
camped
canvassed
captured
carried

carted
carved
cashed
cast
catalogued
catered
caused
celebrated
centralized
certified
challenged
channeled
charted
checked
chipped
chopped
chose
circulated
cited
claimed
clarified
classified
cleaned
cleared
climbed
closed
coached
codified
collaborated
collected
combined

commanded
communicated
compared
competed
compiled
completed
complied
composed
computed
conceived
concentrated
conceptualized
concluded
condensed
conducted
conferred
confirmed
confronted
connected
consented
conserved
considered
consigned
consolidated
constructed
consulted
contacted
contributed
controlled
convened
converted

convinced
cooked
coordinated
corrected
correlated
counseled
counted
covered
created
crossed
cultivated
cured
curtailed
cut
danced
dashed
dated
debated
decentralized
decided
decreased
defended
deferred
defined
deflected
delayed
delegated
deleted
delivered
demonstrated
denoted

descended
described
designed
detailed
detected
determined
developed
devised
diagnosed
directed
discharged
discovered
dispensed
displayed
disproved
distributed
diverted
documented
doubled
drafted
drew
drilled
duplicated
earned
edited
educated
elevated
eliminated
embellished
embraced
emphasized
employed
emptied
endorsed
enforced
engaged
engineered
enhanced
enlarged
enlightened
enlisted
enriched
ensured
entered
entertained
enticed
enumerated
enveloped
equipped
eradicated
erased
erected
escalated
escorted
established
estimated
eulogized
evacuated
evaluated
examined
excavated
exceeded
excised
executed
exempted
exercised
exerted
exhibited
expanded
expedited
expelled
expended
experimented
explained
exposed
extended
extinguished
extracted
fabricated
facilitated
familiarized
farmed
fastened
figured
filed
finalized
financed
finished
fixed
flew
flushed
focused
folded

forced
forecasted
formed
formulated
fortified
fostered
found
founded
furnished
gathered
gave
generated
governed
graduated
granted
grasped
ground
guaranteed
guarded
guided
handled
hauled
headed
helped
hired
hunted
identified
ignited
ignored
illuminated
illustrated
imagined
imitated
immersed
immobilized
imparted
impeded
implemented
implicated
implied
imposed
impressed
imprinted
improved
improvised
inactivated
inaugurated
included
incorporated
increased
incurred
indicated
indoctrinated
induced
indulged
inferred
infiltrated
inflated
influenced
informed
inhabited
inhibited
initiated
inquired
inserted
insisted
inspected
inspired
installed
instilled
instituted
instructed
insulated
integrated
intensified
interceded
interpreted
interrogated
interviewed
introduced
invalidated
invented
inventoried
invested
investigated
invited
invoked
isolated
issued
itemized
joined
jolted
jostled

journeyed
judged
justified
kept
keyed
kicked
kindled
knew
knocked
labeled
laced
landed
latched
laughed
launched
learned
leased
lectured
led
left
lengthened
leveled
liberated
lifted
limited
limited
limited
linked
liquefied
liquidated
listed

litigated
lived
loaded
localized
located
locked
logged
looked
lubricated
made
magnified
mailed
maintained
managed
maneuvered
manufactured
mapped
marched
marked
marketed
massaged
mastered
matched
maximized
measured
meditated
melded
melted
memorized
mended
mentioned

merged
met
minimized
ministered
missed
mistook
mitigated
mixed
mobilized
modeled
moderated
modernized
modified
modulated
moistened
molded
monitored
motioned
motivated
mounted
moved
multiplied
nailed
named
narrated
navigated
negotiated
neutralized
nominated
normalized
notarized

noted
noticed
notified
nullified
obeyed
objected
obligated
observed
obtained
occupied
offered
omitted
opened
operated
opposed
orbited
ordered
organized
originated
overcame
overhauled
overruled
oversaw
overtook
owned
paced
packed
padded
paid
painted
parked
participated
partook
passed
patched
paved
peeled
perceived
performed
permitted
persuaded
perused
petitioned
photographed
phrased
picked
pieced
piloted
pinned
pinpointed
pioneered
pitched
placed
planned
planted
played
pledged
plugged
pointed
polished
popped
posed
posted
postponed
poured
practiced
praised
preached
predicted
prepared
prescribed
presented
preserved
pressed
pretended
prevailed
prevented
printed
probed
proceeded
processed
proclaimed
procured
produced
professed
programmed
progressed
projected
promised
promoted
prompted
promulgated
propagated

propelled
proposed
protected
protested
proved
provided
publicized
published
pulled
pumped
punctured
purchased
purged
purified
pursued
pushed
qualified
questioned
quieted
quit
quizzed
quoted
raced
radiated
raised
raked
rallied
rammed
ran
ranked
rated

rationed
rattled
razed
reached
reacted
read
realized
reaped
reasoned
reassured
recalled
recapped
received
reciprocated
recognized
recoiled
recollected
recommended
reconciled
reconsidered
reconstructed
recorded
recouped
recruited
rectified
redeemed
redesigned
reduced
referred
refined
reflected

reformed
refreshed
refunded
refurbished
registered
regulated
rehabilitated
rehearsed
reimbursed
reinforced
rejected
rejuvenated
related
released
relieved
remained
remarked
remembered
reminded
removed
rendered
renegotiated
renewed
renovated
rented
reorganized
repaid
repaired
repealed
repeated
repelled

replaced
replenished
replied
reported
represented
reproduced
requested
required
rescued
researched
reserved
resisted
resolved
responded
rested
restored
restricted
restructured
resumed
retained
retired
retreated
retrieved
returned
revamped
revealed
reversed
reverted
reviewed
revised
revitalized
revived
revoked
rewarded
rigged
rinsed
ripped
riveted
roared
roasted
rocked
rode
rolled
roped
rotated
rounded
routed
rowed
rubbed
ruled
rushed
sacrificed
said
sailed
saluted
salvaged
sampled
sanctioned
sanitized
satiated
satisfied
saturated
saved
savored
scanned
scattered
scheduled
scored
scoured
scouted
scraped
scratched
screened
scrubbed
scrutinized
sealed
seamed
searched
seared
seasoned
seated
secured
segmented
seized
selected
sensed
sent
separated
served
serviced
set
settled
severed

shaded
shaped
shared
sheared
shelled
shelved
shifted
shipped
shocked
shopped
shortened
shot
shouted
shoved
showed
showered
shunned
simplified
simulated
situated
skated
sketched
skipped
sliced
slipped
sloped
smelled
smiled
smoked
soaked
soared
socialized
softened
sold
solicited
solidified
solved
sorted
sought
specified
spent
spirited
split
spoiled
spoke
spotted
squeezed
stabbed
stabilized
stacked
staffed
staged
staked
stalked
stalled
standardized
started
stated
steamed
stepped
stocked
stood
stopped
stored
straightened
strapped
streamlined
strengthened
stressed
stretched
strolled
structured
struggled
strummed
studied
stuffed
stunned
subjected
submitted
subscribed
substituted
succeeded
suggested
suited
summarized
summoned
superseded
supervised
supplemented
supplicated
supplied
supported
suppressed

surpassed
surprised
surrounded
surveyed
suspected
suspended
sustained
swallowed
swam
swept
switched
sympathized
synchronized
synthesized
systematized
tabulated
tacked
tackled
tagged
tailored
talked
tallied
taped
tapped
tasted
taught
telephoned
tempted
tended
terminated
tested
thanked
theorized
thought
threw
thrust
tied
tightened
tipped
toasted
toiled
told
tolerated
took
toppled
tore
totaled
toted
touched
toured
traced
tracked
traded
trailed
trained
transacted
transcribed
transferred
transformed
translated
transmitted
transported
transposed
trapped
traveled
treated
tried
trimmed
tripled
truncated
trusted
tuned
turned
tutored
twirled
twisted
uncovered
undercut
underestimated
underlined
underscored
understated
understood
undertook
underwent
underwrote
undid
unearthed
unfastened
unfolded
unified
united
unloaded

unraveled
untangled
unwound
updated
upgraded
upheld
upset
urged
used
ushered
utilized
uttered
vacated
validated
vaporized
varied
veered
vented
ventured
verbalized
verified
vested
vetoed
viewed
visited
visualized
vocalized
voiced
volunteered
voted
vouched
waited
waived
walked
washed
watched
waved
wedged
weighed
welcomed
wept
widened
wiped
wished
withdrew
withheld
withstood
witnessed
won
wore
worked
worshipped
wound
wrapped
wrestled
wrote
yelled
yielded
zapped
zipped

Don't Listen to Naysayers

Naysayers find dark clouds on the sunniest days. Like vultures circling sick animals, they seek people in stress to make them more miserable. You don't need them. Avoid naysayers because they will pull you down into depths of uncertainty and despair like you've never known.

If you felt unwanted and/or unloved before you met them, you'll feel even worse after a few minutes with them. They'll tell you about bad things and hope you'll feel as bad about them as they do. You don't need this now. Avoid advising them as well. They already have a negative response for you, and will challenge your positive ideas.

While helping others in need provides value and comfort, at this time you must focus on other things. A tough call? Yes. But tune your radar towards those who can help you get back on track with your life and career.

Identify Your Best Qualities

Now get yourself ready for your next position. Learn about your character, your personality, your mannerisms, your speech, and/or your appearance that made you who you were!

- Keep those things that make you an honest, humorous, appealing, interesting, desirable and respected person.
- Get rid of the detractors.

Consider severing some previous relationships. Tough choices? Yes. But to create a new you, you must deal thoroughly with your past and move on. Building the new you won't happen unless you work at making yourself a better person. You must rebuild the image of someone very important to you . . . YOU!

Reading your emotional barometer will help you recognize stressful situations and the symptoms of the problem before you decide the treatment. Change always creates stress. The more events you deal with or the greater the magnitude of one event, the greater the stress. Embrace change as a normal part of life.

Every job has its own stress. A few years ago, we accepted the bad days at work as part of the job. Recent advancements in analyses of job-related illnesses have narrowed our focus on the problem, and we now refer to those job pressures as stress. Don't take the term lightly. If job-related stress caused you significant problems in your last few jobs, then acquaint yourself with the initial warning signs for any future endeavor. You may still pursue the opportunity, but at least you'll know what pitfalls to avoid.

Dr. Gary Couture from The Institute for Advanced Educational Research, Newport Beach, California, points out, "Stress isn't 'out there,' it's in us. You may never eliminate stressful situations, but you can improve your response to them."[6]

---

[6] Couture, Dr. Gary. *Defusing the Stress Time Bomb.* Toastmaster Magazine, Jan, 1991, pg. 23-24.

Along with help from Professor Jessica Reynolds of Clark University, Dr. Couture developed the COPE formula: Control, Opportunity, Pleasure, and Ease.

Control means you perform activities or tasks your way. If work stifles you, remember that your job generally consumes less than one-fourth of your time in a week.

Opportunity exists when barriers don't. For the most part, our own fears and habits keep us from doing something new.

Pleasure means you look forward to the activity. You enjoy and remember it as good. Pleasure provides reward and satisfaction.

Ease gives you the convenience and flexibility in scheduling, doing things when you want to do them. It opens situations and invites possibilities.

Now you can COPE. When stress mounts, don't duck it, tackle it. Take the offensive toward your own satisfaction.

If you haven't done so already, get in touch with some close friends or former colleagues and let them know about your job search. Approach these contacts in a genuine and heartfelt manner. These people can help you more than you can imagine. If you're not sincere, or you carry a grudge against your former employer, they will spot it before you let the world know about it.

Do You Have a Few Minutes?

We've discussed and suggested time management principles previously, but now we're stepping up to the bar and saying, "Give me a shot of time management!"

"Sure thing bud, coming right up!"

Picture this. You're in your office or working at your desk, and someone approaches and asks, "Do you have a few minutes? This won't take long. I've just got a quick question or two for you."

How often have we experienced this? It happens several times every day. Someone wants something we have or wants some information. Other times, we seek out someone else and request his or her time and advice.

If we ask for someone else's time, we don't worry as much about their time allocations or adjustments, as when someone asks for some of our time. Right? If I need you, I'm interested in what you'll say, because I need your opinion. I won't get upset if my interruption messes up your schedule. However, if you need some of my time, I'm very concerned about meeting my committed obligations, particularly if your few minutes turns into several minutes, or requires several hours or days of my time, which I hadn't planned for.

Time management requires a semi-permanent and somewhat lengthy commitment. However, actual events support the exact opposite. A decision about the use of time acknowledges its dynamic nature. For example, a decision made at 8:00 p.m. on Monday might change by 9:00 a.m. the next day. Suppose you take the same route to work each day, which puts you at your office by a certain time.

However, one morning you learn of an accident directly along your route. Taking your regular route will delay your arrival substantially. You make an immediate decision and take an alternate route. So what if you arrive a little later? That's probably better than if you had followed your original course.

You made a time management decision, one that impacted your schedule and reflects the flexible use of time. Therefore, we'll call it time flexibility. Not a revolutionary concept, I'm just suggesting you rethink the use and allocation of your time.

Given your current situation, downsized or almost downsized, you'll likely have enough time to think about the personal, social, recreational, civic, and professional uses of your time.

- Can I learn how to do something new, or perhaps different than I currently perform it?
- Can I improve myself financially, personally, spiritually, or professionally? Can I enjoy the time I spend in this activity?
- Will this activity cause me to change my thinking about issues? If so, how?
- Will the information or items I obtain from this activity assist me in helping someone else? If so, specifically how?

- Can I use this time to enhance or improve my:
    - professional career
    - personal health
    - family's well being
    - status in community, school, or church?

These issues may not cover every situation, but if you can't answer yes to one or more of them, or at least feel good about spending the time required for the activity, then you need to review your participation.

Account for priority you place on these considerations. Prioritize the importance of your:

- personal health
- family's well-being
- spiritual life
- employment or professional growth
- status in the community, school and/or church
- discretionary or extra curricular time

Before making the world's longest To-Do list, remember that unseen forces influence our lives. These hidden, almost unconscious behaviors tip our scales between frustration and fulfillment, pleasure and pain. Most of us go our way each day, allowing these unseen powers to have full control.

Despite millions of dollars spent each year on self-help books and programs related to time management, most don't mention unseen influences like perception of time and personal priorities, which play integral roles in our overall life-work balance. If we better understand these areas, we can more easily assimilate time flexibility into our lives.

In a 1987 report from the American Psychological Association, Dr. Perry W. Buffington presented a summary of some subjects' perspective of time.[7] Over 10,000 people in the U.S., Puerto Rico, and the Virgin Islands were asked to describe if they thought more about the past, present, or future. From the sample, 57% chose a balance between present and future, 33% were more future-oriented, 9% were present-focused, and 1% preferred to live in the past.

Those with future orientations considered themselves *planners*, while individuals with present orientations lived for the moment, and by choice avoided planning or thinking ahead.

Comparing occupations to time preferences, we find the results relate directly to time management. As expected, managers, teachers, and other white-collar types focus more on the future while semiskilled individuals dwell in the present.

People with time flexibility can take and enjoy the future more and usually have a better paycheck and greater life quality in the present. The future remains the big unknown, but by planning for it, we lessen the effects the little unknowns have upon us.

Dr. Buffington shows how a person's time orientation exerts either a motivational push toward success, or a pull toward complacency. A future-oriented individual in a

---

[7] Buffington, Perry W., Ph. D. *Getting It Together*. Sky Magazine, May, 1987.

management position understands goals, deadlines, and squeezes a lot into a very little time.

One with a present or past perspective in a current management role, no matter how many time management classes they take, may never quite grasp the complexities of getting organized. Perhaps this could explain why certain people never quite deliver the results you expect from them.

Time perspective decides how you allocate your time. Priority plays an equally important role. Psychologists say we have a priority base, which shapes our time allocations and controls our quality of life. The good news, we can consciously work to change this.

Research shows that people organize themselves in various ways. A few years ago, researchers using interviews, questionnaires, and other self-reporting techniques of a 120-person adult sample identified four bases: home, work, home/work combination, and social/extra curricular.

The study found home-based individuals organize to maximize their time at home with their families. They don't necessarily do less work than their colleagues, but if they could manage some activities to give them more time at home, they did so. They tend to marry, and place a high value on time spent with families. Many of these people are self-employed, or have jobs allowing them to work from their homes. Compared to other groups, these homebodies seem happier and more satisfied.

Work-based married individuals spent lots of time at work as the center of their personal universe. They produce lots of high quality work. As a result, they tend to make more money than the other groups. They have fast-paced lives. Single male members of this group spend large amounts of time at work, and have less interaction with other groups.

Individuals with a balance between home and work rarely do anything else. Management decisions don't favor home to office or vice versa. They allocate their time in a way giving them the best of both worlds. Research indicates that the quality and quantity of work both at home and office provides little differentiation.

Finally, Dr. Buffington reported those who organize their lives with little thought to home or office prioritize sporadically, based on widely scattered social responsibilities. No single place formed the center of their world. They didn't express high quality or quantity time at home or work, but spent their time around spontaneous, diverse, and numerous social activities. Generally they seemed less content with their lives than any of the other groups. Because of no single focus, priority, or base, they tend to have more problems making time-based decisions.

You can determine your own destiny. You can do things now to start on the road to a happier and more fulfilling life. However, these accomplishments won't happen by themselves. The passage of time won't make your dreams come true. In 1595, William Shakespeare talked about dreams, when, in *Romeo and Juliet*, he said, "I talk of dreams; which are the children of an idle brain; Begot of nothing but vain fantasy."

If you want to get better organized, then you must do three things: First, learn about your perspective of time. Think about and speak openly to yourself about your time orientation. Fully understand where you focus your primary time values. Remember the Cheshire Cat from *Alice's Adventures In Wonderland*, who said, "If you don't know where you want to get to, then it doesn't matter which way you walk."

Next, identify the priority base around which you organize your daily routines, recognizing it can change a little, based on circumstances. Before changing everything just for the sake of changing, analyze the information gathered about perspective and priority base. Decide precisely what you want to gain from changing your behavior patterns.

Finally, to get better organized, use some of the following direct and conscious techniques to maximize your time flexible decisions. Research shows that at home or office, the *system* (meetings, phone calls, paperwork, housework, child care, etc.) takes 80% of your time. A routine of behavioral methods and tricks can help you effectively manage a day's work in 20% of the available time. While most work best in the office environment, some small changes will make them work at home.

Start with the mail or e-mail, using the A-B-C Method of prioritization. An A requires an immediate reply. Handle a B later in the day or week. Give lowest priority to a C. In fact sometimes you can ignore a C entirely. If you assign work to others, use the A-B-C Method for delegation. In completion terms, an A means "Don't do anything until I've authorized it." A B means, "Get on with it and let me know afterwards what you did." And C means, "Get on with it, and I don't need to know what happened." This stops interruptions before they happen. A one-minute interruption can cost as much as 20 minutes to rebuild momentum.

Work on one project at a time, starting with the most important. Don't stop until you reach a legitimate point of closure. If you stop a project early by saying, "I'll get back to it," you won't. If you stop an activity before resolving the current issue. Mark a new date and time on your calendar to pick it back up. MAKE CERTAIN YOU DO IT!

Group your phone calls, and make them 30 minutes before lunch or quitting time. This minimizes shooting the breeze between you and the other party. You can get to the point of the call.

Take two quiet periods each day, not including lunch close your office door and think about some tough issues. Don't accept phone calls. If you don't have an office, take a break away from your work location. Walk around the grounds, or stroll on a different floor. Do this so your co-workers will respect this as your private time.

Make a To-Do list daily. Many successful people carry day timers or daily planners. Record all your notes and you'll greatly improve your productivity.

Regarding the use of your time, don't carry little scraps of paper around any longer than it takes to transcribe the information into your day timer. Immediately throw those scraps of paper away. Record all your appointments and meetings in the planner. Not only will it remind you what to do and where you need to go, but it also serves as a good audit trail of what you actually did. Make sure it becomes part of you. To borrow from Karl Malden, "Don't leave home without it."

Finally, end each day on a positive note. Say good

night to an office staff member whom you don't normally see. Engage a member of the cleaning staff in some social chatter. Listen to some classical or bluegrass music. Make it a pleasant experience. Make it something that gives you the drive you'll need for the next day.

Do you want to make something better of yourself? Guess what? Times have changed, too. Think back to Bob Dylan's 1963 song, "The Times They Are A-Changin'." Dylan knew something magical when he wrote this, that change goes on constantly and change is something we need to deal with.

Remember our new term, time flexibility. Can you increase your flexibility in the future? Maybe you'll list some things you don't do now, but would like to if you had the resources. Pull out all the stops. Let your mind run free. Look over the exercise "Here's What I Want to Do While I Still Can." Sounds final, doesn't it? It doesn't have to. Try this form of brainstorming and I know you'll enjoy it. So just do it. While this exercise may seem trivial, it might avoid one of those stumbling blocks in your path. Just follow the instructions and don't throw the pages away after you finish. They contain the basic framework for the rest of your life.

Where does all this emotional barometric stuff lead? It will help you identify some of your most important needs, interests and transferable skills. Why? So you can target some appealing job areas to upsize your career and at the same time avoid those areas in which you have no interest, or have little value to your future. You need to start your job search process as soon as you know your job may soon vanish.

Listening Skills

Like any skill, active listening takes practice. This section contains some exercises that will help you evaluate your current skill level and improve it. Review these characteristics of the untrained listener and see how many of these items describe you.

Untrained Listener

- Tunes out the other person at the beginning and prejudges without giving others a chance.
- Quick to mentally criticize grammar, appearance, or speaking style.
- Spends time getting ready to talk rather than listening.
- Tends to listen mainly for facts, possibly errors, to pounce on or prove others wrong.
- Tries to take in and respond to everything, even exaggerations and errors.
- Fakes or pretends attention.
- Divides attention and does something else while listening.
- Doesn't work hard at actively understanding what the other person seeks to say.
- Tends to get distracted by emotional words and doesn't control emotions, sometimes loses temper and lashes back.
- Gives little, if any, verbal response.

- Not aware of the talking/listening "speed limits" mismatch. Wastes thought power and gets lost in tangential thinking. Impatient to "get on with it."

Trained Listener

- Defers judgment, more controlled and listens to discover the other person's feelings and situation.
- Pays most attention to content, not to appearance, form, or other surface issues.
- Listens completely first and tries to get every nuance of meaning. Tries to really understand.
- Listens for main idea and disregards minor points.
- Concentrates only on the main issues and doesn't worry about replying to everything. Avoids sidetracking remarks, especially sarcastic ones.
- Recognizes the human tendency to fake.
- Does one thing at a time. Realizes listening requires full attention. Maintains eye contact as much as possible.
- Listens carefully, sorts, gives feedback, and asks for confirmation.
- Feels honest anger but controls it and does not allow emotional reactions to govern behavior.
- Gives affirmative and affirming statements. Invites additional and opposing comments.
- Maintains patience and concentration while listening.

Okay, if you did an honest appraisal, you a have a pretty good idea of the level of your listening skills. Now let's delve a little deeper.

Exercise 3-2: Listening Makes a Difference

Check your listening skills by honestly answering the following questions. See if you use active listening skills to get the most out of your relationships. Since there are no right or wrong answers, check or circle the appropriate responses and make comments if you think they will help you.

1. Do you know at least a little something about the interests of each person you interview, talk with, or have some professional interest in?

Yes __ No __ Comments

____

____

____

____

2. Do you listen patiently to your network contacts?

Yes _ No _ Comments

____

____

____

____

3. Are you generally a cheerful and enthusiastic listener?

Yes _ No _ Comments

____

____

____

____

4. Do you convey both verbal and nonverbal cues when listening?

Yes _ No _ Comments

____

____

____

____

5. Can you refuse another's request without making him/her feel antagonistic towards you?

Yes __ No __ Comments

____

____

____

____

6. Do you offer people the reasons behind your decisions or ideas?

Yes __ No __ Comments

____

____

____

____

7. Do you ask your friends for their opinions? Do you listen to them?

Yes __ No __ Comments

____

____

____

____

8. Do you mix both open and closed questions in your communications with others?

Yes _ No _ Comments

____
____
____
____

9. Are you slow to interrupt?

Yes _ No _ Comments

____
____
____
____

10. Do you actively encourage others to speak?

Yes _ No _ Comments

____
____
____
____

11. Do you paraphrase, reflect, and summarize when asked to do so?

Yes __ No __ Comments

____

____

____

____

12. Do your friends consider you an effective listener?

Yes __ No __ Comments

____

____

____

____

Exercise 3-3: Active Listening Practice

Like any skill, active listening takes practice. With this exercise you can improve your active listening skills. With a partner, choose one or more of the suggested openings below and give your comments, opinions, ideals, ideas, disagreements, and feelings. Make sure your partner records what you say. Your partner needs to *listen* with empathy and not interrupt you.

Allow about two minutes for each response, then

switch roles and allow your partner to do the same. This time, your partner speaks and you keep quiet and write. You'll quickly see how well each of you listens.

When you've both gone through all the openings, compare written notes. This exercise might take an hour or two. Don't rush it. You'll both find the results very useful.

Suggested Openings

- I believe in . . .
- The emotion I find most difficult to control . . .
- My biggest challenge . . .
- I'm afraid of . . .
- The thing that concerns me most about change . .
- When I disagree with someone, I . . .
- In a new group, I . . .
- The thing that turns me off the most . . .
- The characteristic that I want to change about myself . . .
- I am the happiest when . . .

Chapter 4

Keep The Home Fires Burning

If your job loss occurs unexpectedly, you'll feel upset and likely blame yourself for what happened. In most cases, you didn't do anything wrong, so don't waste your time with this.

You probably devoted several years to your job. Remember the days you wanted to stay home, or go any other place than the jobsite, office, or the plant. However, you made a commitment when you took the job. You agreed to show up for work unless physically unable. So why shouldn't the company have the same level of concern for you? You gave them 100%. The very nerve of them throwing you out the door!

Not talking or keeping quiet about your job loss can make things worse. What should you do? You have no job, feel somewhat numb, and not sure which way to turn. If you could see yourself as others do now, you'd probably have a stooped over posture, slumped shoulders, glassy eyes, a drawn expression, and a blank stare. So many questions run through your mind right now, and you don't know which one to try and answer first.

Every so often, emotions of anger and revenge creep in between the questions. They hang around long enough to sway your thoughts back to the workplace. Naturally you feel sad about the loss of your job. However, allowing your sadness to work itself into a vengeful rage won't help. Such a counter-productive approach could lead you to some serious legal problems.

If, after thinking about your situation, you feel you have some legal issues to pursue regarding your former employer, then get some sound professional legal advice. Pay for and get this advice before taking any steps to tie yourself into a court battle with your former employer. Since you will probably need your former employer for future reference purposes, you should seriously consider what impact such legal action will have on your future employability, and on your potential severance benefits.

Even if you win your legal actions against the company, whatever settlement you receive won't supply your financial needs for the rest of your working life, despite the fantasy in your head. You'll find this particularly true if you participate in a class action suit where lots of people participate in the process, as well as in any damage awards. Whether the company admitted wrongdoing or not, it won't likely have serious long-term effects on the company's continuing attempts to remain in business. Even with a few additional dollars of theirs in your bank account, you don't work there anymore. And, they'll probably continue in business for a long time.

Even if the action against the company seemingly had merit at the time you left, the company's legal counsel might have reached an out-of-court settlement, with the company admitting no wrongdoing. In addition, if you get any compensatory damages (money), you may not have the freedom to discuss the amount you received publicly. If you do, you'll likely lose your award, and may even experience further legal action by your former employer for violating a gag order.

If the issues involved go to court, and you win your claim against the company, several years might pass before you receive any money. Additionally, settlements often have strings attached. The overall decision might look good in a one-time bold newspaper headline, but the reality can prove quite different.

You might decide against pursuing legal action against your former employer. If appropriate and possible, reach a satisfactory compromise through out-of-court settlement activities. However, don't do this without adequate professional legal advice. Legal counsel or advice notwithstanding, you'll need to make the final decision. Make it wisely.

Most companies know their legal positions regarding downsizing staff personnel and eliminating jobs. They've done it successfully for several years. They may not handle the initial notification and dismissal process too well, but from a legal perspective, they'll cover their bases. Management calls this game, "Protect the Company's Image." To do this many organizations offer "early retirement," "buy-outs," and "parachute" packages to some downsized employees. By the way, if the company didn't offer you one, you probably don't have a case. The company has no legal requirement to do so. They offered you employment "at will" and you accepted employment "at will." In other words, the company holds all the cards and decides who gets packages and who doesn't.

You can expect to get paid for any unused vacation time, and possibly accrued sick leave but don't count on the sick leave. Companies interpret severance pay differently. As a rule of thumb, you might receive one week's pay for each year of employment. Ask what severance package applies to you and how much money you'll get in your final paycheck.

If the company's severance package includes outplacement services, take advantage of them. If your employer doesn't mention outplacement services, ask if they will provide them. Whether or not you receive them depends in large measure on your former employer's financial strength. Remember, outplacement services won't find you a job or job interviews. However, they will provide you with a place to gather your thoughts, and provide you the tools to help find your next position.

Most companies will include COBRA medical insurance, primarily because they must. The company might offer a very good package, but the personnel and legal departments will have advised senior management on what the company must offer to keep from losing law suits for discrimination or violation of EEOC guidelines and policies.

If they offer you such a package, consider all your options before accepting it. You can bet the company will *always* protect itself. It has little incentive to provide for your continued future welfare.

If your husband, wife or significant other works full-time, you may consider listing yourself on their health insurance coverage. This could save you some significant dollars. Analyze all the options available in such policies. You can't predict your and other family members' health for the foreseeable future. But you can make some educated guesses. Do you or your family members currently have health problems? Do some household members need some significant dental work? Does your health plan cover these expenses? If not, what other options do you have? Though not often discussed, most health plans offer counseling services. As an employee, you may not have considered such a service but you don't work there any more. Perhaps the COBRA coverage provides this. If so, think about taking advantage of it. Outplacement firms might offer some counseling, but not as thoroughly as a professional counselor.

Your desk now belongs to someone else. The company wants you gone as soon as possible, and might pay you to go away. Assuming you agree, decide quickly whether you can accept what they offer and get on with your life.

If you don't have a legal basis for an action against the company, you might say to yourself, "If I could only go back to the office and talk with the boss, I could explain what a good job I've done over the years. I'll bet I can get my job back."

The time for those thoughts has passed. Denial, may lead you astray. If your company eliminated your job, even your most eloquent appeals will fall on deaf ears. Don't waste your time and effort chasing a fleeting moment.

A downsizing victim himself, former CEO Peter Kolben, suggests, "Don't be angry about the past. Just move on and don't bemoan the fact that your job was what you loved and miss."[8]

Kolben continues, "This means you have to accept the fact that you are now assigned to table 10 at a function when formerly you were seated at table one. It also means that on the other side of the coin, you no longer get the feeling that you are in the main stream . . . the same job doesn't exist any more."

However, remember you can use your talent and skills to help other people and companies, too.

Yes, you'll feel sad. If you lose a loved one, or go through a separation or divorce, you need time to reflect and remember the good old days. So grieve, but don't make a career of it. Don't prolong this unhealthy activity. It doesn't pay very well!

A job loss represents an "economic divorce,"[9] according to Barrie Sanford Greiff, a private psychiatrist and consultant to Harvard University's Health Services Center. Financial worries, feelings of depression, low self-esteem, uselessness, and lost identity often fill the hearts and minds of the unemployed and their partners. Anger, hostility and sleeplessness often follow. While the job loss itself doesn't seem to adversely affect children, their parents' emotional reactions can.

Your family and friends remain the strongest support group you have. Deal honestly with yourself and your family. The sooner you tell what's going on, the sooner you can get on with the important things.

---

[8] *Advice for 'Downsizing Victims: Just Move On,* American Banker, October 10, 1994.

[9] *Keep Your Family Strong During A Job Search.* National Business Employment Weekly, June 2, 1991.

Talk with someone you trust to understand your feelings, but who can still offer you sound advice. Perhaps they live close by, or you can call them on the phone. The person you talk with doesn't have to know all the technical details of your job. Actually, it helps if they don't. You need a sounding board and a trusted confidant. Therefore, talk with an outside consultant, a psychologist, psychiatrist, or guidance counselor. Your current health insurance plan may cover the cost, even through your previous employer. If you have to pay for it, do so. You'll find it money well spent.

Outplacement firm services can play a major role in helping get your professional life back on track. You'll have the opportunity to discuss your feelings with other individuals in similar situations, and you'll appreciate what a strong support unit you have through your family and loved ones. While you may have taken them for granted in the past, you'll soon discover their true value.

Ask your partner to help prepare, address and mail inquiry letters, or conduct information searches into companies you've thought about working with, whether in person or on the Internet. Maybe you need some information from the local chamber of commerce, or economic development council in the town where you want to work. Ask your partner to get the information for you.

Don't leave the younger household members out of the loop when it comes to something this important. They have observations and insights about life most of us wish we could recapture. Tell them why you don't work at your regular job anymore. They need to hear the truth from you as soon as possible.

Additionally, they may have an idea you haven't considered. Their suggestions might seem too simple at first, but you may find a gem of an idea easily overlooked. Give them your attention. Tell them what you do each morning to get ready for your new opportunities. Describe some of your phone conversations, acceptances, follow-ups, and rejections. Tell them about the letters you write and what you say. They'll appreciate your sharing the information with them. These kinds of exchanges will encourage younger family members to help in your job quest.

While you might get lucky and find another position right away, don't get disappointed if you don't. To find a new position, it takes about one month for every $10,000 of annual salary desired.

You may spend several weeks or months at home looking for your next position. So lets examine some suggestions for making your job search tasks helpful and enjoyable for everyone in your home. With their understanding and support, you can all pull together in a team effort.

If you consider moving to a new location, ask your younger household members to find information about schools and communities in the new location. They'll jump at the chance to use the Internet, and might know how to find information quicker than you. Let them help you with typing, filing, mailing, and reviewing job ads. You need to do all these things and while you may find this difficult to accept, you might not have all the skills to perform some of those jobs. Admit it now and genuinely thank the person who does it for you.

Establish an office space in your home in a separate room or in an office with a door that closes. Make sure everyone understands that when you enter that space, they shouldn't disturb you as you work to find your next position. It will take all the time and energy you can muster. Keep the family informed about your progress and ask them to respect your efforts. They'll surprise you with how much love they send your way.

If you didn't organize things very well before, get it together now. Get a desk and a file cabinet. Keep your typewriter or personal computer close by. Try to answer incoming daytime phone calls yourself. Answer your mail correspondence with quick responses. Send thank you letters to network contacts and interviewers. Consider buying a fax machine to send query letters, and responses and résumés to potential contacts.

Thoroughly assess your personality traits, skills, and habits, both good and bad, as well as those characteristics that might need some attention.

Begin tapping into your various support systems. Start with outplacement firms and executive search services. Also, look into neighborhood acquaintances, grass-root support groups through a local church or community activity, networking associations like Business Network International (BNI), your local chamber of commerce, and spouse-support groups.

You need to keep the home fires burning. You always had a very long to-do list that took up your time. Things have changed now because of your time at home. While you should fix that squeaking door, a broken window, a weak basement step, or repair the leaking faucet in the bathroom, don't build that outside deck or remodel the inside of the house.

The time demands you thought taxed you before downsizing don't compare to what's coming up. Your wife, husband, partner, children or younger household members will tell you what they need with few specifications about the final expected products or results. They'll want you to provide magic solutions, feed the masses, turn water into wine, and do great and wonderful things in very short order. When the end result doesn't satisfy what the end-user wanted and they complain about it, you'll wish you had your old job back again. Well, it ain't gonna' happen!

Visit and use your public library each week. If you have younger members in the household, take them with you. Teach them how to use the library's research facilities. Introduce your younger family members to the research librarian and ask for a library tour. Depending upon their age, you might consider turning the event into a treasure hunt or scavenger hunt project. Your family members will treasure this introduction for a long time. However, it may take them a few years to give you credit for having done so.

Since the terrorist attacks on 9/11/2001, many companies have laid off thousands of workers for various reasons. Perhaps demand for the products and services delivered by a particular company has dried up. Do the math yourself. Less demand means less income and less demand for labor to produce products and services. Couple that with a slower than expected economic recovery, and you have the ingredients for a phenomenon taking place in the work place today. More Americans put their families ahead of work.[10]

Interviews used to place all the power on the employers' side of the balance sheet. Now some companies can't hire qualified individuals or request longer hours of existing staff members if the company appears insensitive to their staff's family needs. Interviewees know this before scheduling the first interview.

Assuming a match between the individual and the job opening, potential employees openly discuss many issues with the company in question before they consider any offer seriously.

Some issues include: dependent care, flexible spending accounts, flextime, telecommuting, compressed workweek, bringing a child to work in an emergency, elder-care referral services, adoption assistance, and lactation programs/designated areas.

There's a backlash against the profit-making fixation of the late 1990s. Many people who felt compelled to work longer hours to avoid layoffs have decided to prioritize their home involvement, even if it means paying a professional price.

According to many specialists, the economy drives this shift in priorities. During the boom years of the dot-com era, pay raises came easily. Employees willingly worked longer hours in pursuit of promotions and bigger paydays.

With employees changing jobs less frequently, advancement can remain blocked for years. Also, raises don't raise you much and workers realize extra job efforts

---

[10] *More Americans put families ahead of work.* USA Today, December 5, 2002.

don't guarantee job security. Why sacrifice when no good will come of it? Family values move to the top of the priority list. Your family does appreciate your time.

A 47-year old former corporate vice president and consulting psychologist in Atlanta, who built his own home-based consulting practice says it best. "I wanted involvement with my kids, and I had missed big parts of their lives. Now, I have a strong relationship with them."

Chapter 5

The Job Interview

Okay, now let's get ready for the moment of truth, the job interview. Below you'll find a list of interview questions to think about. Some of them may never come up at all. However, you need to have a response for each of them. If the question seems out-of-line or borders on requesting off-limits information, then demonstrate discretion in responding. They may not know they shouldn't ask the question. Understand your position well before telling your interviewer you can't provide this information.

Below, in quotes, you'll find some sample questions your interviewer might ask. Following each question I've provided suggested responses and a brief description of what information the interviewer wants. Remember, most of what they can't or shouldn't ask deals with personal information.

1. "In your own words, describe your background, including birthplace, education, places lived, previous kinds of work, current hobbies and the factors causing you to perform the kind of work you do now."

Your interviewer wants non-traditional information not related to job performance. Ask your interviewer how this relates to the open job position.

2. "Besides formal education, what additional types of preparation or training do you have for your *current* line of work?"

This valid but tricky question requires a careful answer. It may still focus somewhat on you personally. Don't volunteer information not asked for.

3. "To what extent can you transfer your homemaker skills to this job?"

You must have mentioned this earlier or put it on the application form. If you did, you opened the door. Since you introduced the topic, they can ask about it. Therefore, carefully monitor what you say or write before the interview.

4. "What impact has your previous or current domestic environment had on your current employment?"

Watch out for the word domestic. It can get you in trouble fast. Craft your answer carefully. You should ask what this question has to do with your ability to perform the job. No matter how you answer, think about it before you respond.

5. "Tell me how you would introduce and support a new product or service coming onto the market."[11]

This question falls within bounds, has job related elements, and doesn't directly request personal information about you. Prepare answers to questions about your field that ask about real-life job-related situations.

6. "Describe the kind of work you currently perform. What specific parts of your work do you like and dislike? What parts would you change if you could, and how would you accomplish this?"

Don't fear these questions, as they have job related elements and don't get into personal information. As always, listen carefully to the question and stay focused on the issue.

7. "In your *current* work, describe how your employer discriminated against you or sexually harassed you and how you would deal with these issues in the future?"

Unless you have already revealed information about previous employment that had these issues, this kind of loaded question can lose you the job. Stay away from an immediate answer. If you do answer, you'll likely disqualify yourself from further consideration. You need to recognize it as such and ask your interviewer what specific information they need. No matter how they react to your follow-up questions, proceed with great caution.

---

[11] *Interview Questions You Probably Didn't Expect.* National Business Employment Weekly. September 11-17, 1992.

8. "What do you do to stay healthy?"

Not an unreasonable or illegal question, despite the existence of the Americans with Disabilities Act. The interviewer presumes you're healthy, not unhealthy. Whether you have an obvious disability or not, a good response would stress how you exercise several times a week and eat a low fat and low calorie diet.

9. "In your opinion, do you make a fair and equitable wage for the work you currently perform or did perform?"

A fair question, but don't spend a lot on this issue. If you do, it might prematurely box you into a salary issue. Consider answering you believe you make an appropriate wage at this time, but want to know more about the new position's responsibilities.

10. "Assuming you already have or could acquire the necessary skills for some other line of work, what would you pursue and why do you feel this way?"

Watch out for this type of question. The interviewer wants you to stray into areas having nothing to do with the job position under question. Additionally, it crosses over that personal bridge you don't need to cross.

11. "We know about your hard skills. Please describe your soft skills."[12]

Ask your interviewer for specifics. Respond by stating you have the following characteristics: a positive attitude,

---

[12] "Give the right answers to the hiring questions of today." Joyce Lain Kennedy, *Dallas Morning News*, February 13, 1994.

detail-oriented, productive, enthusiastic, flexible, creative, independent, excited, goal-oriented, a quick learner, leader, team-player, dedicated, motivated and efficient. Make certain you can back up these qualities with examples.

12. "How do you spend your leisure time?"

Translation: What kind of person are you? Watch out for this one. What does this question have to do with the job? Show how your outside interests relate directly to the job.

13. "Would you share travel expenses to your interview?"

The interviewer should ask this question before the interview. Don't split job interview costs. Industry standards call for the employer to pay for all recruitment expenses as a cost of doing business. Money goes from the company to you, not the other way around.

14. "The job won't start until you settle in our city. Can you handle your own temporary relocation costs?"

This issue presents a tougher aspect to deal with than the previous question. How bad do you want the job? Does it offer you more opportunities than anything you've investigated so far? Consider starting with a "no," but consider modifying your stance if doing so makes you a stronger candidate.

15. "What do you think of our package of company materials?"

In other words, have you researched our company? A valid request, this may come during a telephone interview.

If you've obtained some company materials to review, make comments about them, or ask one or two questions about something stated in the materials.

16. "Will you work overtime or agree to be on call?"

As long as you understand the job requires overtime requests or on-call status, such a question shouldn't bother you. However, if you doubt the job requires such extra commitment, ask your interviewer about it. If this surprises you during the interview, it could have a lot to do with your decision to accept a job offer, if made.

17. "Why are you here?" "What can YOU do for US?" "What kind of person are you?" "Can we afford you?" "What makes you different from the 19 other people who already interviewed for this job?"

Interviewers won't likely ask you these questions directly, but all of the interview's questions represent these ideas. Know the answers to these unspoken questions and prepare your answers well.

Okay, I'm Done. What's Next?

You've made an excellent beginning upsizing your career. But you have more to do. Should you work for someone else or strike out on your own as an entrepreneur? Your previous analysis, thought and work will help you in the future, no matter which path you choose.

I've focused the later books in this series on your

career selections. As you read the other books, recognize that you can't do it all. Choose the solution that best addresses your needs and wants. Keep your pad, pencil, pen and computer close by. You'll need them all. Good Luck!

Suggested Reading List

Bennett, Steven J. *Ecopreneuring.* New York: John Wiley & Sons, 1991.

Bermont, Hubert. *How To Become A Successful Consultant In Your Own Field.* Rocklin, CA: Prima Publishing, 1995.

Bernstein, Theodore M. *Dos, Don'ts & Maybes of English Language*. New York: Barnes & Noble Books, 1977.

Bird, Caroline. *Second Careers*. Boston, MA: Little, Brown & Company, 1992.

Bolles, Richard N. *What Color Is Your Parachute?* Berkeley, CA: Ten Speed Press, 1996.

Brown, W. Dean. *Incorporating In (several states available) Without A Lawyer.* Concord, TN: Consumer Publishing Co., 1994.

Burley-Allen, Madelyn. *Listening: The Forgotten Skill.* New York: John Wiley & Sons, 1995.

Burstiner, Irving. *The Small Business Handbook.* New York: Fireside Books, 1994.

The Chicago Manual of Style. 13th Edition. Chicago, IL: University of Chicago Press, 1969, 1982.

Edwards, Paul and Sarah. *Working From Home*. Los Angeles, CA: Jeremy P. Tarcher, Inc., 1990.

The English Language Institute of America. *Practical English and the Command of Words.* Chicago, IL: The English Language Institute of America, 1989.

Environmental Careers Organization. *The New Complete Guide To Environmental Careers.* Washington, D.C.: Island Press, 1993.

Gerberg, Robert J. *Robert Gerberg's Job Changing System.* Kansas City, MO: Andrews, McMeel & Parker, 1984.

Horowitz, Lois. *Knowing Where To Look.* Cincinnati, OH: Writer's Digest Books, 1988.

Joel, Lewin G., III. *Every Employee's Guide To The Law.* New York: Pantheon Books, 1993.

Larson, Jackie & Cheri Comstock. *The New Rules Of The Job Search Game.* Holbrook, MA: Bob Adams, 1994.

Mackay, Harvey. *Beware The Naked Man Who Offers You His Shirt*. New York: Ivy Books, 1990.

Mackay, Harvey. *Sharkproof.* New York: HarperBusiness, 1993.

Mackay, Harvey. *Swim With The Sharks Without Being Eaten Alive*. New York: Ivy Books, 1988.

McQuown, Judith H. *Inc. Yourself.* New York: Harper Business, 1992.

McQuown, Judith H. *Use Your Own Corporation To Get Rich.*
New York: Pocket Books, 1991.

Medley, H. Anthony. *Sweaty Palms*. Berkeley, CA: Ten Speed Press, 1993.

Meyer, G. J. *Executive Blues*. New York: Franklin Square Press, 1995.

Olson, Richard Fischer. *When Do I Start?* New York: William Morrow & Co., 1992.

The Oxford Companion To The English Language, Ed. by Tom McArthur. New York: Oxford University Press, 1992.

RoAne, Susan. *How to Work a Room.* New York: Shapolsky Publishers, 1988.

RoAne, Susan. *The Secrets of Savvy Networking.* New York: Warner Books, 1993.

Simon, Alan R. *Downsized, But Not Out*. New York: McGraw-Hill, Inc., 1995.

Simon, Alan R. *How To Be A Successful Computer Consultant*. New York: McGraw-Hill, Inc., 1994.

Tuller, Lawrence W. *The Independent Consultant's Q & A Book.*
Holbrook, MA: Bob Adams, 1992.

Weinberg, Gerald M. *The Secrets of Consulting*. New York: Dorset House, 1985.

Appendix

Glossary

BBS: Bulletin Board System that allows users to hold discussions and make announcements.

Browser: Software for bringing up and displaying Web pages.

E-mail: Electronic messages sent between computers.

HTML: Language for formatting Web pages.

HTTP: The communication rules for the World Wide Web.

Home page: The introductory page of a Web site.

Hypertext: Text linked to other text by clicking with a mouse.

Internet: A massive worldwide computer network.

Modem: A computer accessory that connects to a phone line, allowing communication between computers.

Password: Letters or numerals adopted by an authorized user, providing access to locked systems.

Search engine: Programs that search a set of documents for keywords or phrases.

SMTP: Governs the transmission of e-mail.

URL: Ensures unique Internet addresses for web pages.

Usenet newsgroups: Electronic discussion groups organized by topics.

Virus: A destructive program that invades and infects other programs, causing them to malfunction.

WWW: Provides a network of electronic sites to form a global electronic network for transmitting information in text, graphics, audio or video formats.

About the Author

Marty Morris

Marty Morris, a native of Birmingham, Alabama, has lived in several areas of the United States, with international assignments in England, Iceland, Italy and Saudi Arabia. Marty was downsized a few years ago, and currently advises others on how to prepare for some uncertain occupational times. He began his consulting business in 1995, and speaks to national audiences on Job Search Techniques and Entrepreneurship. With over 30 years of Management Information Systems (MIS) experience, he has on-hands knowledge of MIS problems and opportunities in public and private organizations related to financial, manufacturing, mail order sales, state government, wholesale food distribution, crude oil production, and natural gas transmission applications software.

Marty Morris has a B.S. in Mathematics from Indiana State University, an M.A. in Economics from the University of Oklahoma, holds the Certificate in Data

Processing (CDP) from the Institute for Certification of Computer Professionals, and the Distinguished Toastmaster (DTM) certificate from Toastmasters International.

Over the past few years, Marty's published articles have appeared in *Computerworld*, *The Toastmaster Magazine,* the *Birmingham Magazine*, the *Cahaba River Review*, the *Diebold TAG Newsletter*, and *Agenda: Magazine*, among others. Some of his published pieces also appear in three current book anthologies: *High Lonesome, The Noble Generation Volume II,* and *Home From The Library.*

To order additional copies of
How to Upsize Your Career

Name ______________________________________

Address ____________________________________

____

____

\$9.95 x ____________ copies = _________________

Sales Tax ___________________________________
(Texas residents add 8.25% sales tax)

Please add \$2.75 postage and handling/book _______

Total amount due: ____________________________

Please send check or money order for books to:

WordWright.biz, Inc.
P.O. Box 1785
Georgetown, TX 78627

For a complete catalog of books,
visit our site at
http://www.WordWright.biz

Printed in the United States
26001LVS00002B/13-51

9 781932 196566